Original title:
Spirals of Ivy

Copyright © 2025 Creative Arts Management OÜ
All rights reserved.

Author: Alexander Thornton
ISBN HARDBACK: 978-1-80567-029-2
ISBN PAPERBACK: 978-1-80567-109-1

In the Heart of Nature's Spiral

In the garden's maze where plants conspire,
A leafy dance that lifts me higher.
I trip on roots, then laugh and shout,
The green parade is what it's about!

The squirrels compete in a nutty race,
While the rabbits hop with the wildest grace.
I'm tangled up in a playful chase,
Nature's wit is a glorious embrace!

Around the tree, a vine will cling,
As I hum along to the birds that sing.
They tease the bees, who buzz with glee,
It's a raucous party, just wait and see!

So if you wander where the greenery spins,
Pack lots of laughter and take your wins.
In this swirl of joy, life's a funny show,
Join the twirl and let your spirit glow!

Flourishes in the Silent Twilight

In twilight's grip, the leaves unwind,
A dancing laugh, no worries to bind.
Beneath the moon, they twist and twine,
    Crickets chirp—'Is this a sign?'

The shadows stretch like playful cats,
While fireflies join in silly chats.
A buzz of jokes in leafy beds,
As giggles weave through nature's threads.

Circular Paths of Growth

Around and round, the vines do play,
With no clear goal, they roam all day.
They trip on roots, they sway and spin,
And wonder where the fun begins.

A leafy torchlight parade so bright,
Each twist a jest, what a silly sight!
They blur the lines 'tween right and wrong,
With every turn, they sing a song.

Whorls of Forgotten Secrets

In tangled knots where secrets hide,
The whispers of the leaves collide.
'Hey, did you hear what Fern did last night?'
'Oh, tell me more! It sounds too light!'

With secrets tossed like silly beans,
The ivy crew share clumsy scenes.
In merry chaos, they conspire,
As gossip flows like wild, green fire.

The Lullaby of Twisting Tendrils

Oh, twine and sip on moonlit breezes,
In the shade of dreams, the fun never ceases.
A waltz of laughs, they twist and curl,
'Let's tie our fates, give life a whirl!'

With each little stir, they chuckle in glee,
'Watch me loop-de-loop, then sip some tea!'
In a giggly dance, they sway and bend,
Till dawn shows up, the night at an end.

The Joy of Ensnared Sunshine

In tangled vines, a dance begins,
With leaves that giggle, hiding grins.
Sunbeams trapped in merry sway,
What a game these greens do play!

Whispers from the branches shout,
'Catch the light, oh, spin about!'
Laughter rings in leafy halls,
Nature's jest, as sunlight falls.

Green Portraits in a Gnarled Frame

Framed in chaos, art unfolds,
Nature's canvas, stories told.
A wild curl, a twisty flame,
Who knew a plant could snag such fame?

With emerald strokes and humor bright,
Gnarled trees in a silly fight.
Portraits of life, all askew,
Nature's gallery, just for you!

Secrets Woven in Natural Symmetry

Twisting tales of green disguise,
Nature winks from leafy eyes.
Secrets hide in patterns fair,
Who knew plants had such flair?

Laughter bubbles, vines entwine,
In a puzzle divine, how fine!
Nature's joke, a grand reveal,
Left us chuckling at the meal.

The Climb into Celestial Greenery

Up we go, with giggles bright,
To frolic in the vivid light.
Leaves above, a canopy,
Tickling dreams, come climb with me!

Step by step, the world spins round,
Upward laughs, with joy we're bound.
In the greens, we find our place,
A joyous climb, a leafy race!

Whispers in the Green

In the garden where leaves play,
The bugs have a party, hooray!
They dance on the petals grand,
While I trample on grass, just planned.

A squirrel drops acorns like confetti,
The birds sing a tune, oh so petty.
The flowers giggle in sunlight's haze,
As I wander around in a daze.

Twists of Nature's Embrace

A twist here, a turn that seems odd,
Nature's playing hopscotch, oh my god!
The trees whisper secrets, not meant for me,
While ants march in line, quite a sight to see.

The sun winks as shadows engage,
Curious cats plotting on stage.
With daisy chains woven by luck,
I trip on my shoes, oh what a shuck!

Vines that Caress the Sky

Vines reach up, doing their thing,
They tickle the clouds, oh what a swing!
The wind laughs, a soft gentle tease,
As leaves rustle, taking joy with ease.

Grass blades gossip like old-time friends,
While ladybugs share tales that never end.
The sun sets, painting skies in quest,
A wild jam session, nature's best fest.

Loops in the Garden's Breath

Round and around, oh what a spin,
The garden chuckles, letting me in.
A frog leaps high, landing with flair,
While butterflies swirl in the warm air.

I'm tangled in weeds, what a plight,
The daisies snicker, just out of sight.
In loops of laughter, the petals tease,
As I frolic, trying to please.

Echoes Beneath the Canopy

Under the leafy dome we play,
Giggling under branches, come what may.
Squirrels gossip, casting doubt,
"Is that a friend or a nut?" they pout.

In shadows where sunlight flickers bright,
We dance like shadows, what a sight!
Leaves whisper secrets, oh so sly,
"Grab a snack!" we hear them cry.

With every twist and every turn,
Nature's jokes, we take our turn.
Laughter echoes as we roam,
In this green world we call our home.

As we tumble and play on the ground,
Nature's laughter is the sweetest sound.
With ivy hats and leafy clothes,
We twirl and giggle, who knows where it goes!

Through the Whispering Verdancy

In the green maze, we play hide and seek,
Giggling softly, we giggle and squeak.
Leaves rustle, sharing jokes from above,
"Don't take it too seriously, just spread the love!"

Though paths may twist in odd ways,
We'll find the light, and dance in rays.
A frog croaks like a jester divine,
"If you could leap, you'd be just fine!"

Around each corner, a chuckle awaits,
In tangled vines, we open fate's gates.
So let us frolic, sprightly and free,
In this green world, just you and me.

As moonlight filters through the leaves,
We laugh harder, as the night weaves.
With every step, we make them grin,
Funny stories and laughter begin!

Latticework of Nature's Heart

In a world of green where laughter flourishes,
Vines weave tales the heart nourishes.
A butterfly flutters, gossipy spark,
"If you think you can hide, just look at that park!"

Underneath the towering trees so grand,
Silly gnomes conspire, quite unplanned.
"Who will trip first on this vine so sly?"
Watch your step, laughter soon will fly.

Daisies peek from their leafy homes,
Chasing after mischief like playful gnomes.
We skip and hop in this leafy retreat,
Nature's giggles sound ever so sweet.

A woven tale beneath the sun,
Each twist, a laugh, each turn, pure fun.
As we wander through this playful sea,
Nature's heart beats in harmony!

Emerald Mysteries in Twisting Forms

In a glade where shadows shake,
We dance with leaves that playfully quake.
What lies beneath the twists and bends?
A riddle wrapped in laughter, amongst friends.

Around us spin the tales of old,
Of trickster sprites, both brave and bold.
A mischievous breeze starts to tease,
"Why so serious? Just sway with ease!"

In every nook, a joke takes shape,
As vines entwine, they drape and drape.
We giggle at the sight we see,
Nature's bounty, full of glee.

With every step, the world unfolds,
A quirky dance in greens and golds.
In emerald paths, we will transform,
Join the laughter, a joyful swarm!

Echoes in the Leafy Maze

In a garden filled with twisty turns,
A squirrel plotted, as an acorn spurns.
Giggles arise from the branches above,
As he missed a leap for the nut he loves.

Leaves chuckle softly, a rustling tune,
While toads croak jokes 'neath the watching moon.
A chase begins with a woeful shout,
As a caterpillar winds, roundabout!

Intricate Paths of the Overgrown

Amidst the tangles, a rabbit prances,
Tripping over roots, taking wild chances.
With every hop, he spreads some cheer,
Though he often ends in a bramble's leer.

Worms poke their heads, sharing their tales,
Of muddy adventures and slippery trails.
While fireflies giggle, lighting the way,
For the squirrel and rabbit's hilarious play.

Nature's Helix Unfurled

A vine twirls gracefully, but trips on a rock,
Sending beetles into a comical shock.
They tumble and roll with a soft little thud,
While a ladybug cackles in her cozy bud.

In the warmth of the sun, frogs practice their croak,
Their off-key songs make the lilies choke.
As a snail slowly dances, all slippery and slick,
He beams with pride at his slow-motion trick.

A Symphony of Flourishing Foliage

In a patch where the daisies wiggle and sway,
A hedgehog sings, though he's shy to display.
He mumbles his tune, tucked under a bush,
While butterflies twirl in a colorful rush.

With each playful breeze, the trees start to grin,
As a chipmunk hops in a wild, giddy spin.
They laugh at the clouds, all puffy and white,
While nature's jesters dance through the night.

The Hidden Embrace of Twisting Growths

In a garden where laughter blooms,
A vine tickles toes in sunny rooms.
It wraps around the cat with glee,
While squirrels dance on branches free.

A game of tag, those leaves do try,
As they chase each other up the sky.
Twisted hands reach out for fun,
A leafy party's just begun!

A Tapestry of Nature's Twists

Nature plays a playful trick,
Vines perform their sneaky flick.
They swirl around the wooden fence,
Like dancers lost in pure suspense.

With leafy wigs and leafy capes,
They host a tea for garden shapes.
The butterflies pop in for tea,
As giggles pour from every leaf.

Verdant Curves Underfoot

Step lightly on the winding floor,
Where laughter greets you at the door.
Each twist and turn a joke to tell,
As roots form paths where we all dwell.

With mischief in their leafy veins,
They conjure plots and silly games.
Here, nature's humor threads through earth,
In giggles woven since its birth.

The Veil of Whispered Vines

In a forest cloaked in green delight,
Vines wiggle with a charming bite.
They sneak a hug around a tree,
And whisper secrets just for me.

Their twirls and curls like tales untold,
Warm the heart, just like the gold.
In laughter's shade, we all align,
In the joyous fold of vine-y whine.

Curved Paths of Enchanted Growth

In a garden where green does sway,
The leaves do dance, come what may.
A vine, like a prankster, snickers and twirls,
Playing tag with the breezes and curls.

With each twist, it giggles out loud,
A merry mind beneath a leafy shroud.
It tickles the branches, what a grand jest,
Who knew plants could be so very blessed?

As sunlight splinters through tangled sights,
The world looks better in snickering lights.
It promises mischief in every turn,
Which keeps us laughing, and hearts that burn.

So may we wander where the whimsy grows,
Among the curls that sow silly woes.
For in every bend there lies a grin,
A reminder to chuckle where joy begins.

The Hidden Stories of Twisting Stems

Once upon a time, a stem took a trip,
Telling secrets with every little slip.
It climbed up high, then down with a pounce,
Making all creatures stop and bounce.

A twist here, a loop there, what a sight,
Leaves gossiping under the moonlight.
They giggle and share what they see in the sky,
While encouraging the clouds to say hi.

Petals chuckle at the sun's golden beams,
As they weave tales in whimsical dreams.
A story unfolds with each knot and curl,
In this world of green, magic does whirl.

So if you pause and give ear to the green,
You'll hear laughter hidden, just out of scene.
For nature's a storyteller, funny and spry,
With a flair for the unexpected and a twinkle in its eye.

Breath of the Climbing Canopy

Up high where the butterflies drink from the dew,
A climbing friend whispers its joy, just for you.
With a puff of a breeze, it lifts to the skies,
With laughter entwined, in each twist it flies.

The vines form a buddy, a jester so true,
It wiggles through branches, like playful glue.
'Catch me if you can,' it calls with a cheer,
As it tickles the noses of those that come near.

In the canopy's arms, all spirits take flight,
Where humor grows wings in the soft morning light.
The leaves wave a welcome, so funny and spry,
You'll leave with a giggle, and not just a sigh.

So climb with the laughter, let your worries float,
On vines that rejoice in their merry little coat.
Each tree tells a joke, so don't walk on by,
Join in the fun; let your laughter run high!

Echoes of Nature's Own Design

In a world where the green talks back with a grin,
The branches rhyme softly, where chaos begins.
A joke in the leaves, a pun in the bark,
Swaying and laughing until it gets dark.

Whispers arise from twirls of the vine,
They tease with tall tales of the linings divine.
A squirrel strolls by with a wink in its eye,
'Oh, these jokes are nuts!' it squeaks with a sigh.

Every twist of the stem spins a tale on repeat,
A chorus of chuckles that merry hearts greet.
Plays hide and seek in the crooks of the trees,
With giggles that dance on the soft morning breeze.

So if ever you wander where vines like to coil,
Listen closely and you'll leave with a smile.
For nature's own humor is woven with care,
And laughter is always just waiting to share.

Curved Shadows of Time

In the garden where giggles bloom,
Laughter wraps around like a plume.
Time sips tea with a silly grin,
As clocks do cartwheels, let's begin!

Tick-tock in a wobbly dance,
They spin around, oh what a chance!
One clock slips and falls on its face,
While others roll on in a race.

Wind whispers secrets in the air,
As shadows play without a care.
Chasing echoes through the leaves,
Making mischief, oh, how it weaves!

A sunny smile, a playful jest,
In this twisty, turning quest.
Each moment, a chuckling delight,
In curved shadows, we take flight!

Tangles of Dreaming Leaves

Underneath a twinkling sky,
Leaves conspire as they flutter by.
They whisper tales of woodland pranks,
In ridiculous, leafy ranks.

A squirrel wears a leafy crown,
As acorns tumble, rolling down.
Dreams entwined in a joyous mess,
Chasing shadows with no distress.

O nimble breeze, with laughter laced,
Tickling branches in joyous haste.
Leaves twist and giggle at the sun,
In tangled jests, behold the fun!

Each leaf a star, they break and sway,
In choreographed disarray.
Nature's jesters, on display,
In dancing tangles, come what may!

Entwined Echoes of the Wood

In the cool shade where shadows play,
Echoes giggle through the day.
Mirthful whispers in trees entwined,
Rewind the clocks, see what's unlined.

Frogs wear spectacles, quite absurd,
Ribbiting jokes without a word.
Bouncing sounds off trees with glee,
As the wood sings its own esprit.

Twisted branches make strange sounds,
A symphony in leafy bounds.
The echoes laugh, they tease and jest,
In this woven wood, we're blessed.

Oh, nature's stage, where shadows prance,
Join the chorus, take a chance!
With every rustle, hear the cheer,
In echoes, laughter fills the sphere.

The Dance of Climbing Shadows

In the twilight's gentle embrace,
Shadows shimmy in a playful race.
A viney twist, a silly spin,
Chasing light, where to begin?

With a laugh, they reach so high,
Feet tickling clouds in the sky.
They stretch and bend, in flourishes,
Performing stunts, oh how they wish!

The moon joins in with a wink so bright,
Encouraging shadows to take flight.
They twirl about, in glowing joy,
In this dance, they just deploy.

Each corner of the world delights,
With climbing shadows in their flights.
A playful night, where spirits roam,
In this merry dance, we feel at home!

Petals Twisting into the Unknown

In a garden, a petal took flight,
Twisting and turning, a quirky delight.
It danced with the breeze, a comical sight,
As bees buzzed by, giggling in daylight.

Stems all around joined in the show,
Wobbling and wobbling, oh what a flow!
A humorous twist that made flowers glow,
They spun without care, where winds wished to go.

The Soft Cadence of Climbing Vines

Vines climbed higher with a giggle and laugh,
Mischievous whispers, what a fun craft!
They wrapped 'round a pole, oh what a gaff,
Pretending to be the world's best giraffe!

In the moonlight, they swayed with grace,
Joking and jiving, a leafy embrace.
Each twist and turn, a hilarious chase,
A riot of green in a merry old place.

Circular Dance of Nature's Heart

Nature's heart beats in a circular groove,
Leaves do the cha-cha, they're ready to move!
Roots tap their toes, they're in a smooth love,
While clouds float by, doing their own groove.

The insects join in, all spinning about,
With twirls and spins, they laugh and shout.
Each toss of a petal, there's never a doubt,
That laughter in nature is what life's about.

Green Ribbons Wound in Time

Green ribbons of life, twisted with glee,
Winding and dancing, oh who could foresee?
Tangles of laughter, a curious spree,
Nature's own joke, in perfect decree.

Each bend in the vine tells stories so bold,
Of laughter and joy in the warm sun's hold.
Time ties the knots, like a yarn to be rolled,
In this world of green, humor never grows old.

Patterns of Growth in Moonlight

In shadows swaying with delight,
The green brigade starts its night flight,
Twisting in ways that seem so wise,
Chasing the glow of the moonlit skies.

With laughs and giggles, they intertwine,
Creating knots that stretch like a line,
Some turn left while others veer right,
A leafy dance in the pale moonlight.

Their leafy antics cause quite a scene,
A jumble of green, oh so obscene!
As the stars twinkle with giggling glee,
They whisper secrets, just wait and see.

In the moon's embrace, they plot their game,
Each twist and twirl, oh, who's to blame?
For in this playful, leafy array,
They'll grow their dreams in a cheeky sway.

A Canopy of Climbing Wishes

Underneath the arch of leafy dreams,
Where every vine bursts at the seams,
They stretch and reach for stars so bright,
With hopes sewn in by the sewing light.

Climbing wishes in a tangled mess,
Vines gossip daily, what a success!
They climb and wiggle, a whimsical race,
Sneaking peeks at the world's embrace.

With each twist and each curl they tell,
How a simple leaf can wish so well,
In a labyrinth of joy, so bright and bold,
A canopy of dreams in green and gold.

They giggle as they tickle the sky,
These cheeky vines, oh me, oh my!
For beneath their leafy canopy fair,
Every wish flutters with flair and care.

The Language of the Clinging Vines

In whispers soft as a gentle breeze,
The clinging vines chat with such ease,
From leaf to leaf, their gossip flows,
About the gardener and how he grows.

They speak in curls, in loops, and bends,
Telling tales of where the sunlight ends,
With every twist comes a new debut,
A comedy sketch with a leafy view.

Each vine a clown, in that jolly parade,
With jokes and jests that they have made,
The trees all laugh, they join the play,
In the garden's theater where dreams sway.

From roots to tips, the laughter swells,
With secrets shared in their leafy yells,
In this green amphitheater of fun,
The clinging vines dance, their race just begun.

Verdant Whispers Among the Ruins

Amidst the ruins, where silence creaks,
The green brigade in a whirlwind speaks,
They wiggle through stones, both old and wise,
With leafy giggles that rise and rise.

Their whispers echo in fragments so clear,
In every corner, they bring good cheer,
Covering bricks with a jolly laugh,
Creating art in a vine-like paragraph.

They share tall tales of the sun above,
And plot their next dare with mischief and love,
In a tangle of green 'neath the cracks and the gloom,
A riotous party among the tomb.

With every twist and a nudging embrace,
They cradle the ruins, a wacky grace,
In this verdant fest, oh what a surprise,
Laughter erupts as the old stone sighs.

Climbing Dreams in Nature's Tapestry

In the garden, dreams take flight,
Little ladders, reaching height.
Leaves giggle, in the breeze,
Chasing bugs, with such great ease.

Bumblebees hum silly tunes,
Swinging 'round like tiny loons.
A squirrel dressed in fancy hats,
Winks and twirls, as nature chats.

Ladybugs, in polka dots,
Throw a party, connect the spots.
On each vine, they raise a cheer,
Who knew plants could drink a beer?

Nature's laughter, oh so bold,
Every vine a joke retold.
Climbing dreams, a tangled quest,
In this tapestry, be our guest!

Curled Secrets Beneath the Canopy

Underneath the leafy veil,
Whispers float like a tiny sail.
Roots are giggling, hearing news,
Of raccoons stealing all our shoes.

Frogs in tuxedos croak and leap,
Secrets curled, buried deep.
The mushrooms dance in funky shoes,
While beetles brag of wildest views.

A spider spins a disco ball,
As fireflies answer nature's call.
Squirrels in a nutty race,
With acorns flying all over the place.

Beneath the canopy they scheme,
In the shadows, they all dream.
Curled secrets, laughter, and cheer,
Join the fun, there's nothing to fear!

The Dance of Twined Shadows

All the shadows start to sway,
In a dance that steals the day.
Roots and vines twine hand in hand,
Creating chaos, oh so grand.

Bugs wear masks and waltz around,
To the funny, leafy sound.
Trees join in with creaky tunes,
Making merry under moons.

Lizards leap, adorned in style,
Stopping first for just a while.
The branches play, they twist and twirl,
As giggles echo, flags unfurl.

In this dance, there's no mistake,
Nature's night can surely shake.
Twined shadows play their game,
Join the fun, forget your name!

Winding Paths of Verdant Enchantment

On winding paths, we skip and hop,
Where the playful green vines stop.
A hedgehog wearing cozy socks,
Takes a break from running clocks.

Ferns and flowers share a jest,
As mushrooms wear their Sunday best.
Caterpillars play hide and seek,
In a world so fun and unique.

Each twist and turn, a silly find,
Nature's jokes are never blind.
A rabbit bursts from leafy shade,
At the punchline, plans are laid.

These verdant paths call out our names,
In their laughter, no one blames.
Join the dance, and stroll along,
In this enchantment, we belong!

The Labyrinth of Living Green

In a garden where the green things twine,
A sneaky leaf gives me the sign.
I follow it, but oh dear me,
I'm lost in a maze of foliage glee!

With every turn, a new surprise,
A giggling snail, or blinking eyes.
I chat with worms who plot each course,
While rabbits hop with such great force!

The paths are twisted, the corners laugh,
I tumble down, what a silly gaffe!
But in this riddle, I find delight,
As petals wink at me, oh what a sight!

In this tangle of greens and chuckles,
Nature's humor makes me buckle.
So here I stay, not wanting to flee,
In this living puzzle, wild and free!

Enigmas of the Climbing World

Upward they creep, those sneaky vines,
Crafting puzzles with curious signs.
A creature peeks from leafy confine,
I swear it winked, oh how divine!

Each twist I take, I hear a tune,
Played by breezes beneath the moon.
I trip on roots, a silly dance,
These climbing greens give me a chance!

Laughter echoes through the leaves,
As squirrels debate their acorn heaves.
Can they hear my giggles ring?
In this jungle, I'm the queen bee swing!

A labyrinth nestled in green delight,
With riddles aplenty, what a sight!
In this climbing world, I'll never tire,
For humor thrives where hearts conspire!

Whispers of Twisting Vines

Beneath the boughs where stories blend,
I hear the vines, my leafy friends.
They whisper secrets, oh so sly,
While I just laugh and wonder why!

A twisty path with giggles loud,
In this leafy world, I feel so proud.
With every step, a chuckle grows,
As ivy tickles me with its prose!

The garden's a stage, where I play the fool,
With plants as actors, oh what a school!
We share our laughs below the sun,
In this theatre of green, we have such fun!

So come along, let's take a chance,
And join this ivy jig and dance.
For in the whispers of each vine,
A funny tale could soon be mine!

Embrace of the Green Labyrinth

In a maze that tangles with much delight,
The greens surround, a merry sight.
Each leaf a clue, each stem a jest,
I weave the path, a comic quest!

With every turn, I lose my way,
But laughter breaks the thorns of gray.
A dash of glee on every trail,
As petals giggle in the gale!

Through curly paths and leafy bends,
I find the joy that never ends.
With every giggle, I breathe anew,
In this embrace of the vibrant hue!

So here I roam, a playful sprite,
In this green labyrinth, I'm filled with light.
For every twist, oh what a thrill,
In nature's laughter, I'm blessed until!

Nature's Embrace in Circles

In gardens wide, they twist and twine,
With leaves that dance like a jolly vine.
They giggle as they climb so high,
Who knew a plant could make you sigh?

A twisting path of laughter laid,
With every loop, a funny braid.
They wrap around the fence with glee,
Like sneaky kids trying to be free.

Amidst the blooms, they play their tricks,
Pretending to be nature's mix.
Oh how they tease the garden gate,
While making every critter wait!

In silly shapes, they love to grow,
Like the dance of a green disco show.
With roots in humor, leaves in jest,
Nature's embrace, we love the best!

The Green Spiral of Evolution

In evolution's quirky game,
Green things twist, but none feel shame.
The world does spin a leafy tale,
With plants that giggle as they sail.

They sneak around the garden bed,
With clever paths, they're always led.
From one to two, then three, then four,
These leafy jokers want to explore!

Their roots take steps like little feet,
In a race to defeat the summer heat.
With every turn, a chuckle grows,
As green life waltzes in spiraled shows.

Nature's comedy in every turn,
A show of leaves we live and learn.
Oh what a sight, so quirky, so fine,
In this twisted dance, we toe the line!

Kisses of the Earth's Greenery

Oh, the little leaves that strut about,
With cheeky charms that make you shout.
They blow sweet kisses to the bees,
In a joyful riddle twisting trees.

Whispers float on the summer air,
With every curl, a comedic flare.
And all the flowers nodding near,
As if they share a leafy cheer.

The trunks stand proud with silly grins,
As nature tickles its leafy pins.
With greens that giggle under the sun,
Kisses of earth, oh, what fun!

In each petal's blush, there's a spark,
Of laughter hiding in the dark.
Nature's jesters on a leafy spree,
Dancing in the charm of harmony!

A Tangle of Green Dreams

In the courtyard, a jumble lies,
A tangle of dreams in leafy ties.
They twist and twirl, not quite in line,
As if they've had one too many wine.

The vines are gossiping up the wall,
In a climber's race to have a ball.
Each loop a giggle, each twist a punch,
A riotous dance, a leafy lunch.

The garden's muse in shades of glee,
A mess of greens just wild and free.
Oh life, you're such a tangled jest,
In this crazy mess, we're truly blessed!

So here's to dreams that intertwine,
In nature's plot, where laughs combine.
In this green chaos, we find the beam,
Where every curl births a silly dream!

Tangle of the Living Strings

In the garden, loops abound,
Twisting tales from underground,
A rabbit hops, gets caught in place,
Wearing leafy strands with grace.

The sun peeks through a maze of green,
Whispering secrets, soft and keen,
A squirrel pauses, scratching its head,
In a tangle, it stumbles instead.

Flowers giggle, roots entwined,
Who knows what they've designed?
A ladybug, unsure to fly,
Decides it's best to just comply.

The wind plays tricks with vines that sway,
Dancing with glee, they steal the day,
Oh, what a knot, what a delightful tease,
Life's a riddle, under the trees.

A Dance with the Nature's Embrace

Leaves twirl like dancers in a grand ball,
Spinning and twirling, they never fall,
Frisky branches shake and sway,
Giggling vines join in the play.

A beetle chases a fragrant breeze,
Wobbling wildly with incredible ease,
A bumblebee hums a jolly tune,
Joining the chaos beneath the moon.

Rooted friends share a cozy chat,
'What's the gossip? Did you see that?'
The earth chuckles, stifles a snort,
As nature weaves a silly retort.

Each blossom winks, a prankster's grin,
In this green confetti, all join in,
Life's a lark in this leafy expanse,
Come join the mischief, let's all dance!

Interlocking Fables in Green Hues

Gnarled tales of the vines reside,
Tangled stories they can't hide,
A snail narrates a slow, grand lore,
Of hopping frogs and a bothersome chore.

A squirrel swings from a leafy perch,
Chasing its tail in a ridiculous search,
Roots are plotting a comeback plan,
'We'll outwit the sly, old man!'

The daisies poke fun at the tall sunflowers,
'Look at those giants, they wasted hours!'
In between, a bashful bud sighs,
Wishing for wings to rise and fly.

Nature's yarn spins a curious plot,
Where laughter is plenty but worries are not,
So let us relish this leafy play,
In this verdant realm, come what may.

Journeying Through Nature's Embrace

In the woods, we take a stroll,
Tangled paths and a jovial goal,
A chicken scratches, looking for seeds,
Among the foliage, it often leads.

A bumblebee buzzes a happy song,
Round and round, it won't be long,
A dancing ant joins in the jive,
Making fun of how they arrive.

Trees share secrets with whispers tight,
'There goes the owl, in the moonlight!'
A raccoon giggles, 'I lost my shoe!'
While rolling with laughter, it bids adieu.

With every step, fate takes its turn,
In nature's dance, there's much to learn,
So come along, join this delightful run,
In the embrace of fun, under the sun.

Canopy of the Twirling Shadows

Under the overhead dance of leaves,
A squirrel critiques my silly moves.
I trip on roots while trying to spin,
The tree laughs, 'Oh, where have you been?'

With branches tickling my crazy hair,
I wobble like a chair with no pair.
A butterfly whispers, 'Do you believe?
That nature can teach you how to grieve?'

But I just laugh, the ground's my best friend,
Every tumble's a joke, and I will commend.
The sun chuckles down with a bright yellow ray,
As I flail my way through a grass-filled ballet.

So here I twirl in this leafy embrace,
Even if I tumble and fall on my face.
Life's a merry-go-round, so come take a ride,
In this canopy where giggles abide.

Reverie in Climbing Green

Lost in a tapestry woven with fun,
I climb to the top but fear I might run.
A lizard shimmies, says, 'You're too slow!'
I reply with a grin, 'You don't even glow!'

These leaves are a jungle, a riddle, a maze,
Each twist and turn, like a sitcom's craze.
A mockingbird laughs at my persistent plight,
While ants carry crumbs—what a hilarious sight!

I leap for a branch, miss it by a hair,
My fall is a classic — a slapstick affair.
I land in a patch of daisies so bright,
They giggle and gossip, 'Now, isn't he light?'

In this verdant realm where the laughter grows,
Nature's the jester, as everyone knows.
So I ascend, tumble, and all in between,
In this climbing reverie, forever a teen.

The Journey of Climbing Hearts

We set out on a quest, hearts filled with cheer,
With shoes untied and all senses sheer.
A rabbit popped up to give us a sneer,
'You humans are strange, but I'll lend you my ear!'

Through tangled vines and above dangling shoots,
We high-fived the gopher in our funny boots.
He chuckled, 'You think you can reach past the sky?
But watch out for clouds—they'll make you cry!'

Yet onward we clambered, our spirits so light,
A chorus of giggles erupted in flight.
We slipped on the dew and fell straight on our backs,
While trees shared their secrets in chortles and cracks.

At the top of this climb, with a view so divine,
We shared all our wonders and sipped on some wine.
In this journey of hearts, laughter was our art,
Painting with joy, we create every part.

Cascading Currents of Green

In a whirl of leaves, the laughter cascades,
Each bud popping out like silly charades.
A frog on a branch croaks, 'What's the fuss?'
While I pratfall once more, landing flat on my bus!

The vines twist like ribbons at a joke shop's door,
Where nature's the punchline, and I want much more.
Grass tickles my toes as I skip and I hop,
While flowers chime in, making my giggles nonstop!

A wind from the east joins this jovial spree,
Whispering secrets, 'Come dance, follow me!'
So I twirl with abandon, my arms spread out wide,
As flowers applaud, giving me a green ride.

Through the laughter of branches, the murmurs of stream,
This world is a carnival, bursting with dream.
In cascading currents, joy's always the theme,
I'll be the clown in nature's own gleam.

The Live-Wire of the Wild

In the jungle, monkeys play,
Swinging branches, come what may.
While parrots squawk in silly tones,
The chaos dances, full of groans.

A snake that slips, just like a dream,
Chasing after mice that scream.
Frogs in hats jump with delight,
Making leaps into the night.

Tigers prance in disco lights,
Trying hard to win the fights.
But all they do is miss the beat,
And tumble in a comic heat.

So join the dance, don't miss the show!
In nature's circus, fun will flow.
With laughs and cheers, we cannot hide,
In wildest worlds, where dreams abide.

Boughs of Hope in Twisted Patterns

Beneath the trees, a squirrel scolds,
As acorns drop like little golds.
A raccoon laughs, all plump and round,
While ants parade all over town.

A pigeon tries to strut with flair,
But ends up tangled in mid-air.
While flowers giggle, soft and bright,
They tease the bees till late at night.

With branches twisted up in jests,
The roots below play hide and quests.
And every leaf a tale untold,
Paints laughter on the world so bold.

So sway with whimsy, trees and grass,
Join nature's comedy en masse!
For life's a joke, so take a bow,
Under boughs where joys endow.

Climbing Tendrils of Time

Up and up the vines do creep,
In the garden, secrets keep.
A tortoise rushes—oh, what folly!
While inside, plants throw a jolly!

The sunflowers twist, all full of sass,
Competing with each curious grass.
They make a show, with smiles wide,
While shadows chime, all set to ride.

And somewhere there, a bear named Fred,
Is dreaming dreams of buttered bread.
He wakes with giggles, sprouting so high,
A comedy act beneath the sky.

As petals dance and colors shift,
Life's little quirks are nature's gift.
So climb those tendrils, take your time,
In this garden, laughter's prime.

Nature's Woven Secrets

In the thicket, whispers spread,
As a rabbit hops and then misled.
He trips on roots and rolls away,
A tangled mess—what a display!

The owls who hoot have much to say,
About the mice who like to play.
And faeries laugh, with twinkling lights,
As fireflies join their nightly flights.

With leaves that giggle at the breeze,
And branches shaking with such glee,
The tapestry of life is bright,
In nature's hands, there's pure delight.

So spin a tale of fun and cheer,
Where every creature sheds a tear—
Of laughter mixed in nature's weave,
With secrets hidden, and tricks up sleeves.

Echoes of the Winding Realm

In corners of the garden's maze,
Laughter dances with the haze.
Leaves giggle in the breeze,
While squirrels plot with such expertise.

A chap with shoes two sizes wide,
Trips o'er roots with clumsy pride.
He tumbles down, then starts to wriggle,
As ivy laughs and does a jiggle.

Amidst the twists, a gnome stands tall,
Wearing shades; is he having a ball?
He waves at frogs who think they're men,
In this green jest, the fun won't end.

The shadows stretch, a dance routine,
Caterpillars dressed in vibrant green.
They spin and twirl, a comical sight,
As the moon joins in, oh what a night!

The Fabric of Growth Yonder

The vines weave stories in the sun,
Of sticky leaves and silly fun.
A snail complains a bit too loud,
While ants parade like a marching crowd.

Each twist and turn a secret tale,
Of toppled pots and the ivy's trail.
A hedgehog snores in a leafy bed,
Dreaming of adventures ahead.

Beneath a shade, a frog does croak,
In rhymes that make the daisies choke.
They giggle so, they barely stand,
What a jolly, jinxed little band!

The air is thick with glee and cheer,
As branches rustle 'round the year.
So join the dance, and don't be shy,
In this world where mischief flies!

Whispers of the Green Labyrinth

In a maze where tales are spun,
Laughter echoes, oh what fun!
The bricks are tickled, vines poke back,
While whispers roam the leafy track.

A squirrel checks his acorn stash,
Then slips and takes a leafy crash.
The ivy chuckles, 'What a show!'
As friends befriend the winds that blow.

A butterfly struts, feeling grand,
With sparkling wings, she takes a stand.
But oops! She lands on a sleepy nose,
Who wakes and wonders, "What's that prose?"

Under the arches, shadows play,
Chasing thoughts till the end of day.
The plants conspire, a prank in tow,
In this jungle where wild things grow!

The Living Cycle of Twisting Greenery

Among the twists, where stories sprout,
Plants giggle as they twist about.
A frog in shades rides on a flower,
While grasses chatter, hour by hour.

A bee insists that he can sing,
While ants debate on the next big thing.
They ponder why the moon's so shy,
And ask the stars to tell them why.

Each curling vine a brand new prank,
Decorated leaves in colors dank.
A gnome chimes in with a tale so tall,
Of hats and shoes that are far too small!

So dance beneath the leafy sky,
With every twist, don't deny.
For in this world, where laughter's fled,
Even plants will dance when mischief's said!

Shadows Amongst the Looming Green

In the garden, vines do sway,
A chubby squirrel leads the way.
Tangled limbs come out to play,
Whispers call, 'Is it lunch time, yay?'

Beneath the leaves, a raccoon prances,
With stolen snacks, he takes his chances.
A cucumber roll, oh how he dances,
While critters watch with knowing glances.

A bumblebee buzzes, full of glee,
Mistaken for a friend, not dinner, you see!
The flowers laugh, such humor so free,
In their floral gowns, they decree, 'Let it be!'

A chipmunk hops with bread on his head,
Tripping on roots where fairies once tread.
Nature chuckles, no tears to be shed,
In shadows green, they all laugh instead!

A Pathway Worn with Verdure

The path once clear now climbs and bends,
Ogres giggle as the lizard lends.
A silly dance that never ends,
In the thicket where humor blends.

Through tangled leaves, a rabbit bounds,
With floppy ears that draw loud sounds.
He jumps and twirls on mossy grounds,
And mocks the birds with strange, loud wounds.

A turtle snickers, slow is his pace,
While a crow dives in like a wacky race.
Every step they take is a whimsical chase,
As nature paints smiles on every face.

With each twist and turn, the laughter grows,
A chorus of giggles where chaos flows.
In this green world, anything goes,
Pathway of fun where mischief glows!

Curled Elegance of the Wild

In the thorns, a caterpillar beams,
Wearing shades, he's lost in dreams.
With each tiny wriggle, he plots his schemes,
In a swirl of laughter, nothing's as it seems.

A perky snail with a top hat waits,
Sipping nectar and eating greats.
While ants march by in casual states,
They giggle at him and twist their fates.

Frogs leap, croaking lessons of jest,
Sardonic humor is never a pest.
In this wacky world, they jest and rest,
Curled with elegance, they're surely blessed.

The blossoms chuckle under the sun,
As dragonflies whirl, a wacky fun run.
Twisted together, they dance and shun,
A wild bouquet where all is well spun!

Nature's Grace in Twisted Harmony

In the orchard, fruit hangs low,
A bear sneezes, causing quite the show.
With a tumble, he rolls, oh no!
But laughter erupts, like a river's flow.

A raccoon wears a crown of leaves,
Pretending he's king among the trees.
With every bow, his subjects tease,
'Long live the king! We won't appease!'

A hedgehog stumbles, oh so round,
Trying to dance, he falls to the ground.
The daisies giggle at the sight they found,
In twisted harmony, joy's profound.

As the sun dips low in a golden hue,
Creatures gather, as evening's due.
In this wild land, old meets the new,
And nature sings songs just for you!

The Artistry of Tapering Leaves

In gardens bright where dancers play,
The leaves do twirl, not shy, hooray!
They twine about like tales untold,
With stories fresh but never old.

A leaf with flair in a snazzy coat,
Sways to the rhythm, how it'll gloat!
A giggle here, a laugh from there,
Whispers of mischief float in the air.

They wink and nod as if they know,
That life's a show with a silly flow.
Do pirouettes, don't stop the dance,
Each curl demands a second glance!

So join the fun, don't you be shy,
Let's laugh with leaves, just watch them fly!
For artistry blooms where whimsy weaves,
In every twist, a chuckle breathes.

Curling Paths of Serenity

Upon the dirt, a path so round,
With curls that twist, a joy unbound.
Must they be normal? Oh, what a bore!
They giggle and squiggle, asking for more.

A squirrel jogs past with a nut so grand,
He stops and spins, such a silly stand!
The curves are playful, inviting a race,
With nature's joy, life's a merry chase.

The flowers chuckle, their petals wide,
As bees zoom by, their buzzy pride.
Each turn brings wonders, oh what a spree,
Nature's giggles tickle trees with glee!

So follow the curves, let laughter flow,
In zigzags of glee, let your spirit glow!
For life is a maze of joy and delight,
Dancing on paths that are hilariously bright.

Nature's Infinite Embrace

Join the embrace of the leafy green,
Where nature's giggles are brightly seen.
Each twist and turn finds fun on the way,
Like chubby bunnies at play every day.

The branches play tag with a flick and a sway,
As whispers of wind join in the play.
With every rustle, a snicker erupts,
Nature's own mischief, that happily corrupts!

Curly vines stretch, like hands in the air,
Waving to butterflies, oh, do they dare!
Each bloom a wink, each sprout a tease,
Entwined with laughter in a joyous breeze.

Embracing life is a comical feat,
With nature's humor beneath our feet!
So let us twirl in this leafy spree,
For laughter is the best company to be.

Trellised Dreams Among the Stars

Up in the night, dreams take a stroll,
Trellises holding them, on a dance of the soul.
Stars giggle down, with a wink and a twirl,
While the moon snickers, "Oh, give it a whirl!"

Vines reach up, with a comedic zest,
For every wild dream, they're put to the test.
"Hey, Mr. Star, don't laugh too loud!
We're in this together, let's make Mom proud!"

They twist and they turn, chasing the light,
With dreams getting tangled, oh what a sight!
Laughter erupts from the galaxy's core,
As ivy overhead requests an encore!

Climb higher, dear dreams, don't you retreat,
With every giggle, you're hard to beat.
So trellis those hopes, let them shine and beam,
For life and laughter weave the best dream.

Verdant Curves in Moonlight

Under the moon, leaves twist and turn,
Whispering secrets, they mischievously churn.
A squirrel in spandex, what a sight!
Doing the cha-cha under starlight.

Laughter echoes from roots to vines,
As frogs hold court, sharing their lines.
"Did you hear about the vine that drank?
It woke up knowing how to prank!"

Poking fun with every curl,
The leaves dance, giving twirls.
With a wink and a nod, they flaunt,
A jolly jig, don't you want?

In this garden, smiles abound,
Nature's jesters leap around.
They play tag with the soft, cool breeze,
Sending giggles through the trees.

Nature's Spiral Labyrinth

In a maze, green tends to tease,
As I wander, I trip on leaves and sneeze.
"Is that a bush or just my lunch?"
It charged at me, I gave it a punch!

Hedgehogs plotting in the grass,
Trying to weave, but oh, what a pass!
They giggle low as they twist and weave,
In this leafy joke world, who could believe?

Flowers gossip like old pals, so spry,
"Did you see that branch? It thinks it can fly!"
It sways, it swerves, oh, so profound,
Yet fails spectacularly, falls to the ground.

Each turn I take, I lose my way,
Chasing the whimsy, oh, come what may.
Nature's riddle, laughing loud,
In the green maze, I'm forever bowed.

The Enchantment of Twisting Greenery

A leaf with attitude, oh so bold,
Thinks it's a dancer, or so I'm told.
Flashing its colors, it shakes its stem,
What a performer, a green diadem!

The roots are plotting a little fun,
Holding hands, they claim the sun.
"Tag, you're it!" they yell with glee,
As I dodge between them, oh, can't you see?

Vines playing hopscotch up the wall,
"Can you catch us? No, not at all!"
They giggle and twist, oh, what a jest,
In the garden's party, they're the best.

The petals laugh as they bring the heat,
Frolicking in rhythm, a truly wild beat.
As the breeze plays DJ, we dance and sway,
In this leafy universe, we frolic away!

Convoluted Whispers of the Earth

Whispers curl like fog on the ground,
Where nonsense blooms, hilarity's found.
Roots are tangled in a jolly fuss,
With the worms laughing, "Oh, join us!"

A ladybug with a monocle on,
Reading a book, while twirling along.
"Can you believe the sunlight's late?"
"I say, let's dance while we wait!"

Fungi flaunt in quirky hats,
Hosting parties with the acrobatic bats.
Mushroom jokes and giggly sprouts,
In this wacky world, we laugh, no doubts.

Come find the point where giggles reign,
In nature's twist, we dance again.
Glorious mischief everywhere we tread,
In the greens, we're never misled!

www.ingramcontent.com/pod-product-compliance
Lightning Source LLC
Chambersburg PA
CBHW071824160426
43209CB00003B/204